That Singing You Hear at the Edges

That Singing You Hear at the Edges

Sue MacLeod

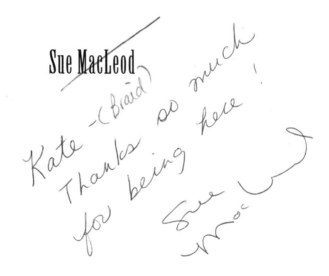

Kate - (Braid)
Thanks so much
for being here!
Sue Mac

George Amabile, Editor

EDITIONS

Cover design by Terry Gallagher/Doowah Design.
Cover painting, *The Three Candles* by Marc Chagall, used with the permission of Image Source International USA.
Photo of Sue MacLeod by Rhonda Knubley.

This book was printed on Ancient Forest Friendly paper.
Printed and bound in Canada by AGMV Marquis Imprimeur Inc.

We acknowledge the support of The Canada Council for the Arts and the Manitoba Arts Council for our publishing program.

National Library of Canada Cataloguing in Publication Data

MacLeod, Sue
     That singing you hear at the edges / Sue MacLeod

Poems.
ISBN 0-921833-90-3

          I. Title.

PS8575.L49T42 2003   C811'.54   C2003-910434-6
PR9199.3.M3343T42 2003

Signature Editions, P.O. Box 206, RPO Corydon, Winnipeg, Manitoba, R3M 3S7

for Jeanna,
and for Sandra and her sisters

Contents

a chorus from another time

The God of Pockets

The God of Pockets smiles on children.
On their thumb-polished chestnuts. And what She,
in her benevolence, sees as their innocent
lint. She sees the lucky penny
drop, knows the hunger
of keys. Knows what the landlord has tallied
on his calculator. Knows the man who sleeps
outside the library. In particular, the flattened
pack of smokes
against his chest. She's held
the knife that carved
the crooked
heart into the tree trunk. The referee's whistle.
The mickey of gin. The wallet, and the picture
in the wallet, and the smile
in the picture. The finally
unbearable weight of a gun
in its holster. Weight of a secret, held in.
She's the god of tide pools. Of harmonicas.
Marsupials. A mother
bounding forty miles an hour
through the flatlands, joey
leaning out over the edge. She knows the way
to a ten-dollar bill
tucked in last winter's coat
on a flat-broke day in spring—like one more
thing that time's
forgotten. And on bright days
when the swing sets and the iron rails
of the monkey bars throw shadows, tall as
office towers spreading to the outback,
the God of Pockets speaks
to children. Run, She says. Take
what you can.

to turn a room smaller

S.M.E.S.

I don't know what took me to that distant
part of town. An appointment? A special
purchase of some kind? Only
that I stepped out from whatever it was
into bright afternoon, and found myself facing
the building where I'd lived
when I was four. That week,
my friend had visited her son in his first
apartment. She'd noticed
how the chairs were set at angles to the wall,
and the countertops wiped down
after breakfast. The same small things *she'd*
always done. And this is what I was thinking about
when I looked across the street
and recognized
the thick glass bricks that framed
the doorway. A delicious coolness
waited past those bricks, I knew, past the serious
grey mail slots. I pictured
a dark red tile floor, rippled
with wavelets of wax, and how those glass bricks
looked like ice cubes, used to make me
thirsty. I thought of a bright red
tricycle, stolen
from beneath the stairs, and how that loss
ate through an afternoon,
right through until supper
when my father came home, when he changed from his uniform
into what he called "civvies," and went out
into the endless, unfathomable
maze that was Halifax, and I knew
he was a miracle worker
for certain when he *did*—he brought it
home. I know what my father looked like then,
not from memory but photographs. Startling—
how thick and springy his hair was,
how it rose up in a wave. His grin with the gap

between his two front teeth. Those
big, stark glasses. A good ten years younger than I am
today. And it's easy to imagine
pulling my little yellow chair up
to watch him with his brush in hand,
the extra paint
dribbling so tidily into the can,
while he wrote my initials
—all four of them—down the tricycle's
long red neck.

—

Driving home, I pass through other
years. Another building,
where the hallways were still floured
with construction dust.
I'd go to the storage room to take out
my toboggan—

        I was thirteen
and it made me want to scream
each time. Not only the sight
of my initials on the curve
of wood, but even the initials themselves
which weren't so much mine
as something *they* had given me, and maybe
more than anything, a certain confidence
which seemed to be inherent
in each brush stroke
as if he thought his lettering
was indelible, as if he thought it could
never be rubbed away.

This is the body, consoling itself

This is the body in solitude
making a companion of itself
& noticing how it makes a companion of itself—
how it's made up of so many pairs.
How right hand & left hand
                              clap
        in *time, time, time*
together, how they work up
a heat.
How fingers entwine
in a gesture of prayer
or a twiddle & whorling
of thumbs. Here's the body

pausing in the doorway, middle
of the afternoon, arms folded   neat
beneath the sullen weight
of breasts...

here comes the rolling:
front foot to   *front* foot
body entering the room.

At times like this the body
is so happy in itself
                        it seems to float
above the mattress, curled
on its side in the wash of light.
Licks of air sift
through the screen.
A wind chime in the distance
is a skeleton of small
bones dancing. Hand alights
on flutter-
pulse of throat.
Now, the knees
tuck further up, calves jostle into place
together. One arm bends

to cradle head sinks deeper
into pillow, eyes grow-
ing heavy&heavier
lids coming
down.

This is when the begging bowl of mind
tips over. And tongue, that old amphibian
in the upper reaches, is one of the last
to stop registering
                        things,
darting like a gecko
on the chamber ceiling, sliding
into molars, fat & brazen
as a bullfrog,
warmth
of tongue its one
            concession
to being human. That, & how it searches
till it finds a loose tooth, jagged edge
or taste of blood just underneath
the surface
& goes back
& goes back there again.

To a friend with her daughter, washing dishes

We speak of old age, and put it away
again: thought on a string.
I sip your good, strong coffee
while we joke about our forties
as a dress rehearsal.
Curtain time ahead! We scare ourselves like kids
at movies. How we do
exaggerate, the way

I do now, convinced
that Lynne's movements are smoother,
more supple than yours
as you work together at the kitchen sink.
And when did her hair become thicker?
more auburn? I watch
her shoulder blades—a pair of wings
could sprout there. And she's the one
best able now to reach
the highest shelf.

There's a shift
taking place, this is just the beginning,
as if something's draining out of us
and into them. Remember how *big*
we were once? We were
giants of women.

With young daughters riding the curves
of our hips, we'd glide through our rooms
collecting *Mommy's keys*, and *Mommy's wallet*.
We were Olive Oyl.
We were Popeye, too.

—

A shaft of light
is falling through your window now

and spreads to every surface.
There are no clear
delineations, not
like in the swimming lessons
when the girls were small. The comfort
of badges, of lanes.
And no bigger miracles, maybe, than this:
that we're talking in the kitchen, still, and our girls
nearly grown. And there'll be no
well-marked corridor to old
from not old yet—only
gradations of light, of heat
touching and leaving
the skin.

But what do I know?
sitting here with my coffee
where I can still play
with an image like this one:
that we're all enrolled in the same
dusty classroom, an old-fashioned classroom,
early afternoon, lingering odour
of paperbag lunches
from home, and they're writing on the blackboard
with their backs to us, our large and shining
children, and the chalk they're using
used to be our bones.

The Curse of Alphabet (and other slight misreadings)

Next to the legal offices of Thomson, Noseworthy and Di Costanzo
is the Sleigh Insurance Office
where the barristers go to get their sleighs
insured against accident, premature
rusting of blades—I imagine
the neighing white horses of Noseworthy,
nostrils flaring in the clipped, British air,
Di Costanzo gliding up with whip in hand, on his breath
a trace of somewhere warmer.

As a girl, I misread
the word "boycott" in my father's *Herald*, mistook it
for "boy scout," hopes raised for an interesting
story. Now I collect like anecdotes
signs I've puzzled over:

> Avoid Costly Breakdowns
> and Head Damage

before I *got* it: *VCR* repair!, the finest
misspellings:

> Bird Houses! $8 Cheep!

> No Dogs Aloud.

And for years
on a house near Five Corners:

> Dr. Fanny
> Office in Rear

Last month, a new sign in my neighbourhood:

Closing November 30th
Thank you for 75 years of business

handwritten in the window of the shoe repair,
a place I never entered—it looked too small, too
personal—and the one time I hesitated, hand
on the doorknob,
I saw the man asleep at his counter; he looked well
into his eighties, chin resting on a knotted
fist, wearing a leather work apron and thin
white shirt. The shoes
lined on the shelves awaiting pick-up
looked like pumps
from my mother's
day, and the tools
were mysterious; there was nothing
that looked digital. It was a surprise—it seemed a trick,
to be precise—that the calendar on the wall
had today's date, this year.

—

To turn a room smaller, stare
at the ceiling. Like the other night,
stretched on my daughter's bed while the two of us talked.
A rare occurrence, now, to be invited in.
Gone: the hammock
of stuffed animals, slung
in the corner, the alphabet poster from elementary
school days—the cursive alphabet, she said one time. I said
the *what?*
Gone: the books with magic wardrobes,
replaced by J.D. Salinger and *Seventeen*.

—

Already, they've torn down the shoe repair.
There's nothing
but a concrete slab,
a parking spot, and I see
it was just that small,
the size of a mid-sized car, where a man spent
the whole of his working life. And his father before him?

I lay on her bed and thought soon she'll be leaving.
On her last night, she may look up
at the ceiling
(where the stick-on stars
got painted over, I meant
to replace them but it never got done)
and think how impossibly small
is this room.
She may take it
as a sign:

    How Small a Life Must Be

that she's grown all
the way to womanhood in a place
this size.

Repetitions, on a daisy

Love me not
for looks or money. Not

for my golden hair,
said Godiva as she turned

to face the crowd. Said Rapunzel
as her prince climbed

closer, closer.
Love me *now*

said the very first boyfriend;
his fingers slid like garter snakes

through dewy grass.
Do you love me? I asked you

and you said I asked
too much.

Bring me your wishes,
three wishes, cried

the fisherman's wife in her meagre
hut. When his last wish

had been squandered,
love me anyway, she said. And don't we all

say? as we stumble to the boarding gate
with rumpled clothes, bad

memories. We pause beneath the sign:
Domestic Baggage.

Love me
anyway, we say.

Love me not
for my sparkling eyes,

not for how my small hand fits
your large one, says the child

spinning away from the carousel lights.
She plugs in her earphones,

adolescence
springing open like a knife.

Don't stop, she calls over her shoulder.
Don't you stop loving me ... now.

—

Did you know? I would have gone with you
to the grove

down by the river
(does the river

have a prescience
of brine?)

to see if we could pick it out
together in the weeping

elm...
the song of one dun-

coloured bird
among the others. A reedy song

through time. If you love me at all
I would have told you, love me for this,

for this which I can never really know
I have. Or am.

Brick Lane

Sometimes the coming together is so sweet
we'd gladly break apart for it.
We fought our way through Hackney
from Stoke Newington to Brick Lane Market
each sway of the bus
that bumped your leg against mine
was a new affront,
tossing together
what ought to be asunder:

you

& me

"we're through
when I get back to Canada."

"Then go," you snapped.
The wheels rolled

over,

over.

Far cry

from the day we sat up top
on another bus
& peered through the rain-streaked windows,
you riding lookout to one side
& me to the other, for a splash of purple
in a grocer's bin—lovers
wanting only for the sky to close
& ingredients
for eggplant parmigiana.
Not eggplant but aubergine
here in your country. I rested

my hand on your knee
& savoured things foreign
but in my own language.

        Water

wasn't pooling in the gutters
    this time
but at the rims of my eyes,
    me   holding down
            the sight
        & sound of something breaking —
not a graceful giving-way like weeping
but unhappiness's answer
to a huge
guffaw.

        Below us
your city unfolded raw
as nerves
& by the time we reached Brick Lane
barbed wire
was strung on many
lower balconies

—

"not four not three oi'll tike"   there were trays of petunias   & you
saying, *why can't you just believe*   " 'AV some lavly marigolds"   lamp-
shades with tassels gone yellow "oi'll tike TWO POUND FIFTY!"   "'ere ya
go, Squire"   the boots they were selling were   *why can't you just believe*
me?   full of holes   *why can't we stop this once & for all?*   "izza vejdibble
chopper, mite"   lava lamps   backscratchers   "cuts sharperana RIzer!"
ashtrays like skull & crossbones   " 'ow kin ya pass it up?"   & then
coming through the crowd a shrunken   " 'ERE ya go"   planet's whole
stockpile of unwanted   "ya won't git a bedder price anyplice lidy, izz-
AL stolen"   a shrunken old man with stubble & rheumy blue eyes
cradling   *why can't you just believe*   cradling   *I love you*   a live
white rabbit in his arms

—

What would I tell you
        if I knew you now?
How handsome you looked in that spring
of your fortieth year?
But those are easy words
when what I mean is elemental: you were
man to me.
I remember the salty
cracked voices of the hawkers
when I started to cry,
when I *began to weep* then,

        "whazzamadder luv?"   "y'awright dear?"

The old man's water-
colour eyes
& the pink eyes of the rabbit—
they seemed frozen
in a snaking line of people
& a squiggle of bare concrete
might have been
                a forest path
we were waiting turns
to take. I turned away

into the good-leather smell
of your jacket,
your arms coming round me,

        "What's he *doing* with the rabbit?"

my lips   brushed
the base of your throat
& you said

        "What is it?
                What is it about that
        that makes you so sad?"

How could you *not* know?
    it was
    everything —
not so much that something could shatter
    our lives
but more the way we go on even after
something has.

I'd tell you
I've long forgotten the cause of that fight
but not the gentle pressure
of your arm around my shoulder
as we left Brick Lane, left
all the sad dresses & miracle
gadgets, caught a bus & rode it
like a thread pulled
on the bias,
the tapestry of London,
the trip home always shorter
than the one away

—

I'd tell you, sometimes
when my hand comes to rest
on the curve of my hip, where the body swivels,
I know that I still carry
how we'd take each other, steer
each other home. Back
in your bedroom, our clothes washed away
with an urgency like summer rain
we moved   together
hard enough   to wear the edges off.

Then, under cool sheets,
the heat of life coiled in our intertwined legs
& your breath on my neck
you drifted into your own view, looking
for whatever   splash
of purple,

              & I drifted back

                      to Brick Lane...

       was he taking it home
          to *eat* it?

                   was he taking it home
                    for a pet?

           did he hold it   for comfort?

        had he *brought* it   to the market
    for the walk?
the sights? for air

I lifted your arm from my shoulder,
rolled in to the gaps in your sleep-heavy breath
& dreamed he was living
in a room just above,
dreamed your street had grown meaner
to meet him, your walls held a chill
& the home-from-teaching clatter
of your housemate
in the hallway
faded to a
shuffle, drifted
into footsteps on the floor above,
a creaking of springs,
the man breathing,
the rabbit
too soft to pick up.

the gathering up of each wave
before its breaking

Swoop like the gulls

It doesn't matter which roof
you light on. All points
lead back to your home
once removed,
your mother's, not quite yours.
You could start with the wishing

with the *wish-wish-wish*ing
of your mother's scrub-brush moving
through the house,
the world, in circles. You'd float
out the screen door & onto the porch,
riding a swell of soapy water
gone gritty & cold. Start

when the road really *is*
like a ribbon

                (glow of dashboard dials,
                  gauges aligning at the proper points)

     unspooled it's come
unspooled & rounding
every bend
the sure black tires of your father's car
rewind it
        rewind all of you
        (father-mother-child-&dog with snout
        against the window for its hiss
     of air)

   carry you
over the old hills
carry you
over home

- 35 -

When climbing mountains after dark
don't   think
of the slow-
motion

                somersault

that waits beyond the guard rail
(husks of cars resting on the bottom,
rusting out)

Think of the time
before guard rails
            when this road was mud, was

                        closed
                        in winter

            your mother, a girl
        when the supply boat came in spring
                                time
        when the ice in the harbour was melting like cubes
        in a glass, in a mouth. Imagine

the place your mother is taking you
home to, the place
you'll never reach.

When mother & daughter discuss
the facts of life

Why did grandma have thirteen children & you only had me *how* could you fit
at the table together *where* did you sleep *is* that a picture of the first little Jake
in the living room *how old* was he
when he died you *really* couldn't leave here in the winter *there was no*
TV *how* could you keep
from going crazy *what* ever happened to Elliot *why* are the bottom
curtains pinned
shut?

—

Apartment buildings never
have a thirteenth floor. Think
of that if you think the old ways
are dead. Now we have choices.
Think of that if you think the old ways
were so romantic. Think of loaves
& fishes, loaves of my mother's bread rising
together, a tea towel spread across the pans.
Jacob was three
when he died of fever. Ten days later, Mama
had your uncle Jake.

Mountains on both sides of us,
no roads in winter to cross them, & not
much more to say.

The water Robbie brought in from the well
would have a coat of ice by morning.
We would crack it. Load
the stove. Sometimes there were kitchen parties.
Can you picture Gordie dancing? Cedric
on the spoons? We'd come home
in horse & sleigh & fall
into a sleep as thick
as snow.

...no, that isn't step dancing you're doing,
that's just foolishness. There are
rules you don't know. And I've told you a dozen times,
Susan, go easy
when a cake is in the oven. One false move
can make it fall. Come here, on my lap.
You're fading
as I look at you. See? It's getting dark out.
When the world outside
your window is as big as sin,
a thousand times bigger
than you are,
there are times to turn away, we knew
when not to let things in.

That blur in the corner

is Elliot, walking
out of the picture. You can catch
a bit of rubber boot, plaid shirt-tail
flapping up the lane.
There aren't many
pictures of Elliot, he didn't want
to be in anybody's
album. "*Me son*," he'd say
every time I'd get the camera out,
"*me son*"—although he never
spoke a mean word I could tell
he meant it— "get away from me
with that thing."

Picture...

what you won't forgive. Picture the moment
you learn the word "alone." You are playing
on the beach all morning. You are nine or you
are ten. You are "swimming," you call it, in the
shallow water. Arms down, supporting—the
rest of you floating. I'm swimming! you say
though there's no one to hear. It's the year
you are learning to swim. You are learning to
skate, in the winter. You are learning long
division.

Picture...

you climbing the steps by the fish shack,
crossing the road, hair wet & bathing suit
gritty with sand. It's the year after Rudy died.
No licks, no brown tail wagging.
Just your mother on the doorstep.
She takes one look & says, Stop!
Strip that suit off before you come in.

This year you're supposed to be a big girl
but you're crying like a baby.
Someone will see me!
She says, no one will.

Picture...

the basin of water
your mother throws over
                you, naked & pleading.
Picture the moment your uncle drives by.
The long maroon sweep of his car &

the volley of beeps, his arm out the window.

      Picture...

      your uncle Jake, laughing. Picture
      your mother waving back & laughing too.

How the world might sound

Aunt Grace has shaken
the sand from her towel, & here
she is raising both arms in a gesture
like worship
to hang it on the line.

There's a coolness
you can almost touch
rising from the ground beneath her.
She has slipped .
her old black sweater on
—it holds her shape
the way her arms still hold the heat
of afternoon, & the tingle
that fills every pore when you've been
in the sea

        —later, we'd lie with our eyes closed
  & the lapping of water
  & a kind of wooden creaking
            kind of rope &
    wooden creaking
that always seemed to come
from somewhere
          added up
to how the world might sound
from inside a barrel, or a wooden hull
between any two ports
at some moment in time, while the
sun
bore
down.

They buried the 40s
in my grandmother's well

They buried the 30s, 20s, buried
everything that came before them.
Tap-ilif... *tap*-ilif...
thank you, they said
as they threw
the hand-tooled bridle in
& the whinny
of the dappled mare

They dropped
in the last lump
of sugar, they dropped in the last puff
of woodsmoke & their dirty
bins of coal. They dropped in their world
war one medals, & felt
the turning over
of their fathers, far
across the sea

An kewan shyair, they said
in a moment of confusion:
the Atlantic, the ocean to the west.

They dropped
the old green icebox in
& it fell with a thud
to the bottom

making ready
for the Westinghouse, the Frigidaire,
these men
still strong & hardy
in their nineties, these women

in their homespun cloth,
how certain they were
of a brighter, an easier

life for their children
for their children's
children.

They threw in the *kew*-uch, the cave-
haunting monster. And at last,
the bloodstained washing

of the *Ben*-nee-*i*,

spirit of mothers
who died   giving birth

no suffer... no suffer... no more

They threw in the kerosene lantern.
The long black night.
The silence.
And slipping through their fingers
& they couldn't even know it
was

        the rhythm
        of a water pump,
was
        the clop-clop-alonging of hooves
        on the high   way
was a crate
        of eagle cries

I picture them, shaped
by the thin, crumbling soil,
by the gathering up
of each wave before its breaking.

The ankle-sting of thistles, bleating
of lambs. This was what they had & it was all
around them, reflected
in the flecks of green blue brown they saw
in one another's
eyes. I picture

the old women squinting
in the sunlight, & the old men
spitting.

Smack oo *vair*... they chanted.
It is good... It is good...

Smack oo *vair*... their voices spread
across the water

They stood with hammers swinging
from their callused hands. Ready
with the six-inch nails, the weathered
boards. They tossed
the rotting apple in,
& the worm inside the apple

Ha-*mee* sha-*geen* sha-*goot*, they said.
You're telling me.

We won't be needing
that no more.

Didn't they warn her
away from the cliff?

(i)

Didn't they tell her
not to wander? Don't
the grass blades form
an undulating
chorus, as she moves chest-
deep among them, don't they
whisper:
back   back   back

And the women darting back
& forth
from wash-house to the clothesline.
Won't a remnant
of their voices
                    carry
on the wind
& call her in
to jelly sandwiches, the rising shape
of morning? Doesn't
just one woman turn
& see a speck of red hair gliding
through the meadow:
smaller, smaller

flame.
And the waves against
the cliff wall, don't they
frighten her? ex-
plode at her: go
home girl! home girl! home!

When the clods of earth begin
to loosen, does she turn & grab

the world? As she starts
the long slide down:
a final glimpse of laundry
twist&turning as it
beats like holy fury under sheer
blue sky

(ii)

The fisherman who found my cousin Julia
saw a heap of bright cloth on the rocks
& rowed in
closer. The details have grown
dim with time. I wasn't
born yet—I don't know if she became
a living miracle.
Though I seem to

remember
they took down
the mirrors, so she wouldn't
see her swollen face,
run screaming from her skin.
I seem to remember
she cried when they touched her, she
cried when they cut off
her long, tangled hair.
child, returned
from the edge

To summon the Angel of Rescue

keep your fingers crossed against
eventualities. Think of your grandmother,
baby after baby after, turning them out
like turnips from the rust-
brown soil, turning them out
to the world. *Mama!* they cried
in a cawing
like crows. Think how big the sky
was then. The tide kept
coming, coming.

To summon the Angel of Love at First Sight
look both ways
at every tree & city
corner. Brush your hair a hundred
strokes, repeating: You never know *what*
to expect. Try to imagine

what *was* it? about *him*?
that lifted her up, her straw
hat in one hand, & carried her over
from the Catholic side
of the mountain
to the starkly
Presbyterian. Over his threshold &
straight up the stairs. Think
of slats

of sunlight on the oilcloth
floor. Their brief, first summer.
The storm windows off & the bed warmed
with light. Think of the long dark
hair of your family's women.
Think of curtains kicking in a

rising breeze, think of salt
breezes, of sand
drifts, think
swept.

To banish the Angel of the Early Frost,
guard your house
against her sharp-
tongued sister—rumoured
to take shape among
the tangled bedsheets—
Angel of You Made This Mess, Lie *Down*.
Think of your grandmother's face
at the window, growing
fainter after every
nervous breakdown, looking out
on her adopted view.
The rosary she clung to
like a life-raft. Church she married
out of. Church that turned her out

for all those years, until
the new, young priest came through the fields
to find her.
Didn't give—but asked—forgiveness.

One summer you will be arriving,
driving past his church, & you'll
pull over. It's the summer
after your divorce
& you have such a need to believe
in tenderness.

To summon
the Angel of Kindness
imagine that new priest—still young,

still kneeling—& your grandmother
not yet beneath the well-clipped lawn,
but tugging her white gloves on
over swollen knuckles.
The tickle of powder. The tilt
of a hat. And her, tremulous. Be
tremulous.
Remember how you saw her
colour rising through
her veil, her veil of net.

She looks back

& sees her mother
in the distance—tiny
set of head &
shoulders, growing
out of *her* mother's

rose bush.

Something white
in her hand—it must be
the dust cloth—she seems to be
waving:

hello   good-bye   I love you

She could be calling
a truce
for everything that ever
has gone, ever will go
wrong
between them.
She could be polishing
a rose.

Three warnings

1.

One day
on a road or
a teeming city street
maybe
on another continent

you'll notice
the smell of salt, a trace
of wild roses,
feel the old yellow grass at your ankles
& know
    this is no
           mirage.

The sea might be slate grey
at this moment, or
come-hither
blue purple.

It will have been a long time
since you swam

2.

MacEwan's old barn is still standing
(just barely)
at the crest of the hill,
clear blue sky around it.
And you will turn away
as from a mirror

3.

Of all warnings
this should come first:

you look back to see your mother
in the distance,
to call some small remembrance
across the fields, &

she isn't there.

She gave me

formula because the doctor said she was too weak to nurse. It was a record Ontario heat wave. It was 1955. And my father swore he'd never put her through that again. She gave me her mother's name, Mary Susan, turned around. And a painted wooden cow that mooed when you pulled on its cord. It was called "Molly Moo Moo" & I ran & hid. She gave me the window seat whenever I wanted. At the end of one summer we took the train together: Cape Breton back to Toronto. She gave me a colouring book to amuse me, but the vibrations made my hand shake & I whined about it. Later, they gave us blankets & I fell asleep with my head in her lap.

She gave me

a shake & whispered my name. *Susan*, she said, *wake up. Susan*, she said, *look at the lights of Quebec City*. I was four, so it wasn't anonymous big-city lights to me then. It was fairyland. Lights of Que-*bec*. We were stopped on the tracks & the world was soft & dark around us. All but the glitter. Then the train began to roll.

She gave

a stuffed animal I really wasn't through with to my cousin from the big, poor side of the family even though I cried. She gave me Vicks Vap-o-Rub when I had a chest cold & she'd rub it in so hard I'd want to scream: *I wish you loved me!* She gave me a doll called Chief Flora, being proud of things Scottish & Cape Breton, but once when a Yonge-Street receptionist said, *you sound Maritime*, she lied. She gave me Barbie & Midge & Barbie's little sister Skipper. She gave me countless accessories including an old heart-shaped locket with her initials, *I. MacL*. At eight I put my favourite of the Beatles in it, but later I couldn't find anyone that small.

She gave me

Duncan Hines brownies when I came home from school. She gave me her dark eyes, which sparkled, but not her nipped-in waist or straight Scottish nose. Those, like her secrets, she kept to herself. She gave me no lessons in cooking or housework. You could eat off her floors & she was nervous of the mess beginner-hands might make. She gave me money & sent me to Johnny's when we got to Ingonish one year. I walked along the rocks to get there, took a Pepsi from the cooler, knowing someone would be bound to say, *Is it Isabelle's girl?*

She gave me

        a black velvet jacket, a blue Princess telephone & a call every day when I was 18 & out on my own. By then she was giving me gifts she didn't understand: a tripod, a telescopic lens. Across from the camera shop I focused on the doorway like an expert, tried to show her how to bring things close.

She gave me my birth

        certificate & a permission slip I needed for a liquor store ID. I laughed when she put quotation marks around ID & To Whom it May Concern. She gave me a dirty look. She gave me a dresser I'd wanted from an antique store downtown. My father said we'd never make it up those stairs. *Oh go away, Jim*, she told him, *the women will do it ourselves*. So we struggled up the staircase of that big, old building, my apartment door winking at the top. We grew hungry & tired & from downstairs came the smell of someone cooking curry, there was nothing to latch onto, the drawers kept falling open, we sat on the landing & laughed. She was 60. I was 24. We didn't know about the cancer then.

        —

The black velvet jacket

        she gave me, I wore long after she had died. I looked good in black velvet. Above its soft darkness my eyes shone like hers did. Cities at night.

When you walk on the rocks,
& the sea
yields up no answers

To walk on these rocks
is a play in three acts, your life
unfolding

—

pebbles roll
beneath your feet
(marbles, with an edge)

the grind&scraping
of the surface you're disturbing
as these
small
rocks/rub
together:

earth beneath you moving
fast as you
can move
on top

—

when you come to the edge
of the sea

the rock
formations sleep

like beasts, you climb
the haunch

of one/ stroke
      bone-white/ bone-yellow/
      bone-smooth/
      rock

settle
      in
      beside an echo
      chamber, water
      rushing into low-scoop cavern

      sucked
      back out:

                              the *glug*

                                    & Thunder

                        ━

when you come to the edge
of your mind
the sea has churned
away your questions

            (can you even name
                        its colour?)

                        turning
                  back to middle ground

            rocks as big as
            knapsacks, skulls

(relearn
a first secret:

no two   are the same)

                    you're paying
                            more attention
                    to your foot-
            falls than you have
                    since you were very small
                        (& may again, should you grow
                                relatively
                    ancient)

                    (will the next rock stay in place
                        & will it hold

                    you)r every move a conscious
                                move & yet so quick

        you make it

            every step
        an act of faith, an act
        of balance.

Self-portrait, as sea-shell

conch

1 *any of various large marine snails (sluggish or slow moving)*
not getting much done, my mother scolded, my head in the clouds
having a spiral shell I am her daughter, I am her mother's daughter's
daughter, I come from Ontario, come from Cape Breton, come from the
Hebrides, Isle of Lewis *roughly triangular in outline and with a wide
lip often curled back* like a breaker, roaring in to shore *revealing
a smooth pearly lining* for shame, she said, learn to be modest
2 *the shell of a conch*: home, living on after the creature has
abandoned *used as an ornament* don't leave me here collecting
dust, I hear her calling *or for making cameos* no, I tell you, hold me
to your ear.

A woman is making

herself. She is taking the lines
of her body from the hills across the water, her breath
from salty air. She is panning for tears in the deep
cold sea, & heating them up
to make them ready, warming
her hands at the stove. She wants fire, she wants wind
to burn a lifeline in-
to doughy palms like these.
A woman is frightened. Her fears rise
like curlicues of steam, they turn to mildew
on the kitchen ceiling. She is swaying
a child on her hip, & her swaying
is the *lap...lap...lap*
of water on a shoreline
& her swaying
is the clattering & rumble of a subway train, cradled
in its track. A woman is meeting the eye
of a needle. She is sewing the uneasy pieces
into one. She is folding her memories into a box
small enough to slide into
an apron pocket.
A woman can make herself
small, she can slide
into the pocket,
curl herself up in her memory box
until she is back in the first
of her childhood apartments, on her knees & rocking
in the platform chair. The curtains are blowing.
On the balcony, her mother is shaking a dust-mop,
banging the handle on the crusted metal rail,
backing into the room—her own
dust-mop shuffle.
"There," she says brightly. She
pulls the door shut so that nothing
blows back in.

that singing you hear at the edges

Before the wreckers come,
Carry away
The lightning-bulb of sun.

—Pat Lowther

When Night meets Thread & Needle
& lies down among the bedclothes

This night begins in scraps—blue velvet
sky & water. Timeworn, but indispensable to eye,
to skin. As colours fade, my needle makes
a path for figures. Their movement
lending focus, shape.
The birds by now are knots to hold the trees in place.

And that singing you hear at the edges?
My mother. Her sister, Grace.
On their way home from a dance. This thread, pulled
from a story someone told me.
And from Moon, who poured a path-
way to the beach & set them

laughing, full skirts gathered up in fists & bare feet suction-
cupping cold wet sand. And reeled them
up the ladder, to the loft of this old fish shack... so
to sleep. These tassels you can roll between your fingers
are the *lap...lap...lap...* of each small wave, as
clear, distinct, as certain as a sister's breath

beside her. Shots of silver for the gaps
along the beams. They are 19. They are 21
or 22. The nap, like seagrass, parts
to make their way.
Sleep, my child. Pull this night around you. Even
as the sky grows light, starts bleeding

into vivid pink. To lavender. The start
of blue. Moon still out, a pale swatch.
Their shoes are swinging
from their hands. Feet wet with dew.
And this is where my needle
pauses. A stitch before this shadow

in the distance, on the doorstep turns
to Papa, Papa quaking:
the shame you have brought on this house!
And Moon, the younger sister
who began the trouble, wills herself invisible
& fades away.

Lay the raw
silk of a dawn like this against your cheek.
Their legs are young & strong, arms resting
on each other's shoulders. The needle & the breath
held. The first birds about
to sing.

Especially after rain, the gulls

Earth is a stadium
& the crowd is going wild tonight, the crowd

wants blood. Why
are they squawking so loudly

out there on the island? No more
fish guts on the breakwater, or tossed

off the side of a boat
for them? Or were they always like this, & I just

don't remember? It sounds like
something has to give, something has to happen.

The stadium roof will blow off tonight
or the gulls will pick the land-

scape up, yank it free
of the bedrock that holds it, pull away

what's green & fine,
roots dangling like the stuffing of Salvation

Army furniture.
Especially after rain, the gulls

are flapping (unhinging)
wings in unison, against

white bodies, preparing
to carry the island away

in their scavenger beaks & take it
...where?

Newsworld Tonight

after Elizabeth Bishop

Tonight, after a lengthy absence, we return to this
remote and desolate country.

The pocket of civilization which was clinging to
existence here at the time of our last report has
vanished. The reasons, at present, are unknown.
Environmental mishap? Escalating civil strife? Or
genocide? at the hands of an external force.

external modem

Our crew is here tonight because our radar has been
intercepting signals. They are believed to originate in
this low-rise industrial building, which we now
approach on foot. Our aerial reconnaissance informs
us that this structure is equipped with a row of
rooftop lights. Listen!

merp-merp-merp merp-merp-merp merp-merp-merp-merp

After a brief pause, this ten-note signal will repeat
itself without any variation. Although we can find no
entry point into the building, it is almost as if a
survivor were trapped in there, attempting to send a
message out, but unable to get through.

halogen lamp

There is no moon tonight, but visibility is good
because of a clear white light which illuminates part of
the landscape. It is suspended on a black metal tower,
as tall as many of our skyscrapers, and resembling a
gantry crane. Its efficient design and large scale are
further proof that progress was beginning in this
undeveloped country at the time the natives perished,
or made their escape.

A quick perusal confirms that signs of human life—
and death—which our earlier correspondent noted,
have now disappeared from the scene. The closest
facsimile to a border or barricade—always a marker of
human society—is a staggered row of elongated metal
loops, coloured gunmetal grey. Several are joined, as if
the natives were building a large, chain-link fence
when they were mysteriously interrupted.

paper clips

Some of you may recall the dugout, or "nest" of
strangely contorted corpses which disturbed our
correspondent. Thankfully, this has been cleared
away. If memory serves me, the bodies were those of
foot soldiers, in the camouflage uniform which was
then being issued in this tiny, war-torn land. Our
anthropologists inform us that soldiers of this
regiment fell out of favour by the end of the twentieth
century, and were banned from almost every public
place.

(ashtray)

Due north from the spot where their ashy grave
existed stands a large holding tank. A fuel tank, we
presume. Its height exceeds its circumference, and it
appears to be made of a cardboard-like substance. A
closer inspection reveals faded lettering, most of it
illegible. But wait—the first three symbols appear to be...
t... i... m...

coffee

Circling back, we face east, where a large escarpment
rises. But look! The escarpment—whose elaborate
terracing was once the only accomplishment of these
isolated and backward people—has been swept away!
Clearly the result of a natural disaster, or a human
undertaking of tremendous scope.

(typewriter)

In its place lies a plain—flat as prairie—most of it
taken up by horizontal grey slabs. Although they lie in
heavy shadow they appear, from this distance, to be
marked with etchings of some kind. In fact, the entire
plain resembles one of our modern, suburban
cemeteries, but on a larger scale.

keyboard

We now grow increasingly aware of a structure which slipped our notice earlier: It seemed to be part of the heavens. We now see that it is man-made—a screen of some kind—and that its presence subtly dominates the land. It emits a faint, staticky drone and has the backlit quality of a twilight sky. Occasional lightning-shaped flashes of colour float across its otherwise blank face.

monitor

As we approach, we feel a sense of expectation, as if some type of show is about to begin, the best "seats," as it were, reserved for cemetery residents. All joking aside, we expect that our questions will be answered as we move toward the coloured lights and the ceaseless, low white noise.

No one like us

She was walking along her new street one night in what her agent called
a recently discovered kind of neighbourhood, going to the store where
they sell cigarettes one at a time & know everyone's name & brand,
when she noticed a light in a window upstairs, the curtain was open, the
wall was a turquoise *too* turquoise a colour like the very orange powder
that comes in Kraft Dinner, the pink of cotton candy or something else
with too much sugar or too much whatever, mascara, or Jesus, she was
thinking how it only takes a patch of colour on a wall like that to tell
her this building hasn't been done yet, no one like us lives here

& thinking of her two small sons how they wouldn't know that yet, they
wouldn't know it from seeing the man who came into view, she could
tell he'd been handsome once & still had a certain charm, sinewy arm
raised, a gesture to someone just out of her range, like the pack of
Export A's, the Olands she imagined on the table—a man who might
give them some money for candy, who'd dig in his pocket, liking their
smiles & not thinking at all of their teeth, she was thinking

not without nostalgia of the ache in country music, of neighbours on
the front porch on a summer night & thinking of her two small sons &
things she didn't know at their age: certain scientific facts like the
reason for rainbows & how we divide & divide in our cells.

This is a poem where words are the underpaid workers

This is a poem
for the helping words: if, and, or, in, to…
written in sympathy
for their cause, their desire
to step out from the shadow
of the rushing verbs, the nouns as fat
as capital. This is for weeknights
when helping words gather in the basement
of the local church:
"My name is The, and I'm a co-dependent."

This is about the uncelebrated power
of words like these. About telling
the truth, or *a* lie. Going home; going
into a… home.

This is a poem where words
are the underpaid workers
who give you a sponge bath, and bring the small articles
you call for. The ointment. The bedpan.
A little something to make you
more comfortable. They're the ones whose tenderness
or cruelty matters
in those hours
before your body becomes
"the body." It is their cushion soles your loved ones follow
down the corridor—"this way, please"—
to claim you, in the end.

The day Elizabeth Montgomery died

I was folding towels & pillow slips, peeling
small garments from the ribs of wrong
companions, matching red sock yellow sock purple sock blue.
The TV was going always
going at the laundromat

Elizabeth Montgomery today succumbed to cancer

Had she stretched out her still-lovely arms? To never again
stand blonde & beaming
in a Sixties kitchen. Never again
roll her eyes at Endora. Never again do that
thing with her nose

She came into the hearts of millions of Americans

& my heart too. The announcer built momentum:

> *She was a good suburban witch,*
> *struggling to repress her powers.*

The day Elizabeth Montgomery died, I wheeled home
my wet & heavy laundry. Felt it shift
like an animal over the curbs.
Stayed tuned in
for the johnny-jump-ups poking through pure
gravel. The lightning
bolts of sidewalk cracks. Hushed
conversation of leaves. Three girls playing
double-dutch stopped short
of levitation.

Unloading my basket I felt it again: my old anger at Darren,
& at *her* for giving in to him. Darren and his advertising clients.

Samantha, I would know now
how to tell her: they would steal
your magic. Sell it back.

The day Elizabeth Montgomery died, my bones were also
older & my nose was still
not twitching. For now, it was enough
to hang my laundry
on the line, red sock yellow sock purple sock blue.
Reel it into the sky.
Every piece a flag, a sign:

Sam, don't they know?
the streets are full of us.

Thirteen ways of looking
at a clothesline

I

Looking down affords a particular
view of *up*.

The shape I duck away from
as I round my corner
doesn't
      loom , doesn't
      swoop
as it did in shadow,

attached to no heart
beat, no wing
beat, un-
still eye.

II

How do I show you how it is
to hang this laundry out?
First, to pluck
      that lone marauder
from the clothesline,
fold it into checkered
dishcloth in my hands.

III

A woman finds a black towel
in her bathroom, reaches
out to touch
        a bat.

Framed
in her window pane:
a pale sheet,
flapping.

IV

How do I show you how it is
this fresh June morning?

A photo, if I had a photo, couldn't
catch the gracefulness—my
black dress, black shirt, black jeans
gliding
just above the lilacs,
leaders
in a funeral procession.

A photo, if I had one, couldn't
catch the scent of roses
through the fenceboards, nor the essence
—partly smell and partly feeling—
of water
drops dissolving
from these linens in this
basket in my
arms.

V

Thin men of Halifax,
you're thinking I can't see beyond the laundry
in my own backyard.

But *I* have seen

clothes-
lines stretching window   sill to   window
sill across a cobbled
alley,

strung
from sycamore to
      sycamore
above rust-
coloured chickens.

VI

In May,
a line of summer dresses.
Yellow. Melon. Lavender.
Each one
a day she reels in,
pulls it
from the blue.

VII

Even with no birds in sight
a certain
choreography.
Each dancer in its own
air current   lifts and

      dips
to its own
rhythm. When the wheel
      turns
they shrug, sashay
in unison, a chorus
line.

VIII

In a high wind
when the full skirts
balloon
and sheets turn
into parachutes,
I wonder: When we spun
around the room
together, was he holding me
up? or down?

IX

That was no
dark tablecloth edged in white
suspended
in the lane
at dusk,

but the robe
of a twenty-foot
judge.

X

My neighbour and I wave
across the fence to one another.
We are hanging out the water.
We are wavering
to each other through the very light
blue sheets.

XI

Hear the squeal
of a clothesline, a few
lives away.

XII

The line snaps in two like a belly flop.
Weight of the world. And even
as she runs
to collect wet linens
from the dusty ground, she feels
the pressure gathering
behind her knees, the sweet
relief of all
that buckling.

XIII

How do I show you
how it is to bring the laundry in
this soft June evening?

Each pillow
slip
      sways
left, sways
         right
and at the end the mourners
dance.

a chorus from another time

Day-nighter

> Let me leave quietly by Gate 29
> and fall asleep as we pull away from the ramp
> into the tunnel.
> >   —Gerald Stern

Let me go by the train
and not in the air-lift of air-

plane. Let me not
leave the bright, tarmac world
with its equipment and rotating lights
but the world from the backdoor:

fire escapes, service lanes heavy
with clotheslines. Small
yards where eternity
clings to the hands
of an old man, an immigrant
always, caught
in the planting of roses. Let me go

low to the ground and catch
a glimpse of backyard decks and hooded
barbecues. The season
not yet quite upon us, but these towns are so valiant
in their expectations. This banner,

   Amherst Animal Shelter Picnic

snaps
and flutters in the greening
park, though I can almost taste the moistness
of the round black clouds above it. Let me go

slow enough to catch
the tiny gesture. A cat springs
from a fence and streaks, grey tail bushing,
through the grass
toward its destination:
a hand, a screen door
opened. Let me take

one final chance to savour
small absurdities:
a crisp white back porch
      severed
from its crisp white house
sits, tilted, on the sloping lawn (a finger lost, still
pointing).
Does it hold
somebody's rubber boots? The hook
with their matching
yellow slickers? Let me go

not for a long time
and when the time comes, let me weep
like that old Jewish poet on the streets of New York,
calling out *for the faces I love, the names I can't forget.*
Let me separate my two
sad hands, release
my expectations into the rumbling
world of this

   Day-nighter: Montreal
                 to Halifax

A few rows back
someone asks, where
can I find some traditional houses?
Do you think I'll be able to see
a fisherman, bringing in his catch?

As we pull into another
red brick station, a girl
stands where the platform meets the grass. She hugs
her sweater around her, arms
surely goosebumped in such changeable
weather. Keeps pushing a strand of dyed
hair from her eyes, searching
the windows for a face.

Dissolution

for Richard

How to think about anything
other than you, driving the car
and bringing
my fingers to your mouth,
how you take them, one and then
another, teeth tracking my knuckles, tip
of your tongue on the pads
of my thumbs, where identity
is traced. I lay my two hands
on the keyboard now, say: write.
How to write about anything other than your
arms coming round me, breath
on my neck, your lips which search
for mine, then draw away. (I turn
toward you.) How to
turn toward anything other than you when you
tease. How to tease out an image
other than you, moving
above me. How to move
through my day-to-day
life, as if the breath is not
knocked out, knocked in and
out of me, my knees not gel
as in a drugstore novel, as if
I wasn't living in this state
of dissolution: in this state of being liquid.
I walk through my rooms
and melt down in an image that rolls
through my mind: a flash
of dark chest, the crisp
white undershirt you lift
above your head in one swift motion.
How to lift anything
other than layer after layer down to skin
against skin, till there is nothing
left between us. Who are you, anyway?

We look at one another. Don't want
the whole answer. Won't enter
that space which allows for the distance,
the difference
between us, and for your laugh, your private
male laugh when you're done.
How to do anything
other than think about you
driving the car, and me
sliding my finger
into the slit at the top of your glove.
How to stop myself from thoughts
of going further
down to your palm
where your life line is laid, heart
line is laid. How to think about anything other
than laid. Sex, you say, can make us dumb
if we do enough of it. We break
the surface for a breath. But this
romance is rooted in our minds—well, *isn't* it?
So I must tell you
I am brilliant in my state
of being liquid,
like water in the white-capped bay.
How it breaks
against the rocks and shapes them even
as it takes their shape. I imagine
water rushing through the caverns now,
filling every cranny of the tide pools with
what later, in the golden
light, will show no sign of wildness,
only grace. How to hold on to
the grace of your hands
cupping my face,
or in their chaste gloves on the wheel
now (outside the year's first snow
is falling) as you steer us
into just our second season.

Drive, I want to tell you. I could undress
your hand for miles. And you've said you could live
on the taste of my skin. But this
is where conditions can turn
treacherous, the water harden
into ice beneath us.
Drive, I want to tell you. Take me
home.

Dispatch

Now that we find ourselves deep
in this place, there are some things
I may be needing.
So tear yourself away

and lope along the wide
grey streets. Blow down my door again.
Pad across my kitchen. Find the cup
I used to drink from when my lips were made
for speaking

...see you! rooting
through my cutlery, my paper clips and tokens,
the world of tools and implements.
I used to be a member. Remind me

of the time I breathed
so cheerfully such thin, unscented air.
The years I used to cook
things before eating.

At the tide pools

On the shore my mother came from, the departing tide
left pools in the depressions it had carved
into the dinosaur-
scape of rock. Pools with snails clinging

to the edges. Pools in certain light so clear, at times
you wouldn't see one till you'd walked
right in. Deep enough
to soothe my mother's aching

feet, to bathe
my rubber babies. I didn't know then
that the moon pulls the tides
as it would later pull on me, like all

the other women. When the moon is just
a thumbprint in the morning sky
I'm at the office, working in my cubicle. It reaches
through the concrete walls and fields

of electricity. I feel it tugging
deep inside:
pebbles held fast in their bed of wet sand, while the water
rushes through.

And now, the moon
tugs feebly. Now—wildly. Now... not at all. A rhythm going
crazy. Across the broad expanse
of sky, I can almost see the guide ropes, frayed.

One day they'll snap, and I'll be left
like shoreline where the tide's gone out and won't
return again.
It is then I will find myself back

at those tide pools, walking alone.
I'll let the moon pour down
its milky light on me
and hear the water roar.

I've come to fill my pockets up,
not weigh them down. To comb
that shore for anything
that's luminous, or white.

Especially for a woman, reading

Especially in the afternoon when light slants
through the window, grazing her cheek on its way to the page.
For a woman who appreciates that kind of light
for reading. Especially in mornings, when coffee makers
groan. When everyone else is still climbing, still hand-
over-handing their way
up from dreams. For the book
that fell into the bath
and was fished out—*quickly*. For the line
that swam before her as she fell
asleep. In stolen time: the check-out line, the way to work.
In fits and starts of traffic, in the press
of bodies. Especially
for anyone who's ever missed
her stop. For anyone who's laughed out loud while reading
in a restaurant. Or ever thought of writing
to a stranger:
You told my story. How did you know?

Especially for a teenage girl whose touch
turns bookmarks into ash. And so
she uses rubber bands, a roll of tape, a stray sock, a receipt, or *my* book
to hold *her* place open. Who won't
come to supper till she finishes her page.
For a grandmother I know
about, who stirred with a book in one hand. For everyone stirring
with words in their hands. For anyone who's ever grasped
a book in two hands.
Hold your breath, and crack it open.
For books that have burned to be written. Books
thrown into the fire
because supper wasn't ready, or her chores had not been done.

For anyone who's ever had anyone
tell her:
All that reading makes you think too much.

Especially when the leaves against the window
are a chorus from another time.
When evening comes, a woman stretches one curved arm to reach
the light behind her. She is reading
while the birds take roost, and punctuate
the branches. Reading till her book is finished. Reading
like a girl.

Notes and Acknowledgements

I would like to thank the editors of the following journals and anthologies, where many of these poems have appeared: *The Antigonish Review*, *Arc*, *Contemporary Verse 2*, *Event*, *The Fiddlehead*, *Grain*, *The Malahat Review*, *The New Quarterly*, *Other Voices*, *Room of One's Own*, *TickleAce*; *Body Language: A Head-to-Toe Anthology* (Black Moss Press, 2003), *Coastlines: The Poetry of Atlantic Canada* (Goose Lane Editions, 2002), *Landmarks: An Anthology of New Atlantic Canadian Poetry of the Land* (The Acorn Press, 2001), *Rip-Rap: Fiction and Poetry from the Banff Centre for the Arts* (Banff Centre Press, 1999), *Vintage 2000* (Ronsdale Press, 2000), *Words Out There: Women Poets in Atlantic Canada* (Roseway, 1999).

In the year 2000 "The God of Pockets" won first prize in *Arc*'s Poem of the Year contest and "Especially for a woman, reading" placed second in the League of Canadian Poets' National Poetry Contest.

—

"Thirteen Ways of Looking at a Clothesline" is after Wallace Stevens' blackbird poem, as "Newsworld Tonight" is after Elizabeth Bishop's "12 O'Clock News," (*Elizabeth Bishop: The Complete Poems 1927-1979*, Farrar, Straus and Giroux, 1983). The quotation on page 79 comes from "Let Me Please Look into My Window," and the italicized line on page 80 from "The Faces I Love," both from *This Time: New and Selected Poems of Gerald Stern* (Norton, 1998). The epigraph on page 62 is from Pat Lowther's "Let the Wreckers Come" in *Time Capsule: New and Selected Poems* (Polestar, 1996).

In "They buried the 40s in my grandmother's well," the Gaelic phrases are written in phonetic English. The correct Gaelic spellings are as follows: thank you: *tapadh leibh*; the ocean to the west: *An Cuan Siar*; the cave-haunting monster: *Ciuthach*; the spirit of mothers who died giving birth: *bean-nighe*; it is good (that): *'s math gu bheil*; you're telling me: *tha mis' ag innse dhut*.

The poems in Section II are in memory of my mother, Isabelle MacLeod Suffidy. "S.M.E.S." is for my father, James Suffidy, with thanks for all the miracles.

—

I am grateful to the Canada Council for the Arts and to the Nova Scotia Arts Council for funding which supported me while many of these poems were being written. My gratitude also to the Hawthornden Castle International Writers Retreat in Lasswade, Scotland; and the Sage Hill Fall Poetry Colloquium, Muenster, Saskatchewan, and, once again, to the Nova Scotia Arts Council for funding my trip to Sage Hill.

I thank Daphne Marlatt and Doug Burnett Smith for their help with the poems in Section II. I also thank everyone in my poetry group, and especially Margo Wheaton (as always) and Brian Bartlett and Deirdre Dwyer for their generous readings and response. I am grateful to George Amabile, my editor, for his skill and directness, and to everyone at Signature Editions. My deepest thanks to the following for their editorial acumen and more: Richard Kurtz, for seeing; Jill MacLean, for her friendship and for steering me to Signature; Julie Vandervoort and Sandra Barry for their sustaining enthusiasm for my work. Finally, thanks to Jeanna Greene, my daughter, for inspiring me and for suggesting Chagall.

MEMBRE DE SCABRINI MEDIA

Québec, Canada
2003